ABT

P9-ECX-815

4/09

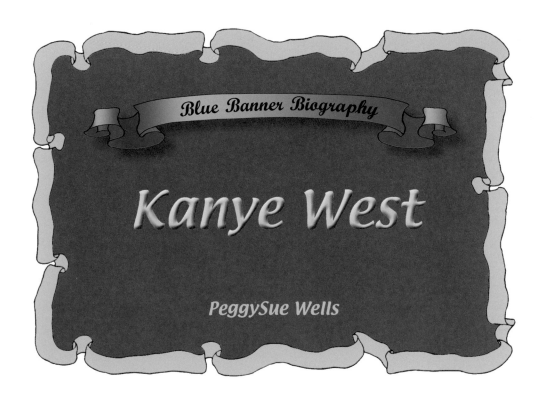

Blue Banner Biography

Kanye West

PeggySue Wells

P.O. Box 196
Hockessin, Delaware 19707
Visit us on the web: www.mitchelllane.com
Comments? email us: mitchelllane@mitchelllane.com

Mitchell Lane PUBLISHERS

Printing   2   3   4   5   6   7   8   9

Blue Banner Biographies

Akon	Alan Jackson	Alicia Keys
Allen Iverson	Ashanti	Ashlee Simpson
Ashton Kutcher	Avril Lavigne	Bernie Mac
Beyoncé	Bow Wow	Brett Favre
Britney Spears	Carrie Underwood	Chris Brown
Chris Daughtry	Christina Aguilera	Christopher Paul Curtis
Ciara	Clay Aiken	Condoleezza Rice
Corbin Bleu	Daniel Radcliffe	David Ortiz
Derek Jeter	Eminem	Eve
Fergie (Stacy Ferguson)	50 Cent	Gwen Stefani
Ice Cube	Jamie Foxx	Ja Rule
Jay-Z	Jennifer Lopez	Jessica Simpson
J. K. Rowling	Johnny Depp	JoJo
Justin Berfield	Justin Timberlake	**Kanye West**
Kate Hudson	Keith Urban	Kelly Clarkson
Kenny Chesney	Lance Armstrong	Lindsay Lohan
Mariah Carey	Mario	Mary J. Blige
Mary-Kate and Ashley Olsen	Michael Jackson	Miguel Tejada
Missy Elliott	Nancy Pelosi	Nelly
Orlando Bloom	P. Diddy	Paris Hilton
Peyton Manning	Queen Latifah	Rihanna
Ron Howard	Rudy Giuliani	Sally Field
Sean Kingston	Selena	Shakira
Shirley Temple	Soulja Boy Tell 'Em	Taylor Swift
Timbaland	Tim McGraw	Toby Keith
Usher	Vanessa Anne Hudgens	Zac Efron

Library of Congress Cataloging-in-Publication Data
Wells, PeggySue.
  Kanye West / by PeggySue Wells.
    p. cm. — (Blue banner biographies)
  Includes bibliographical references, discography, and index.
  ISBN 978-1-58415-677-2 (library bound)
  1. West, Kanye—Juvenile literature. 2. Rap musicians—United States—Biography—Juvenile literature. I. Title.
  ML3930.W42W45 2009
  782.421649092—dc22
  [B]

2008008058

ABOUT THE AUTHOR: PeggySue Wells is the author of many titles, including the *What to Do When . . .* series and, for Mitchell Lane Publishers, *Fergie* and *Soulja Boy Tell 'Em*. A popular speaker, she has written screenplays, books, and curricula. Her magazine articles appear nationally. She's a member of the Remedy.FM advisory board and the Christian Performing Arts Fellowship, and is a coordinator for the Tweener Ministries international teen writing competition. PeggySue is the button-popping proud mother of seven children. For more information, visit her web site, PeggySueWells.com.

PUBLISHER'S NOTE: The following story has been thoroughly researched, and to the best of our knowledge represents a true story. While every possible effort has been made to ensure accuracy, the publisher will not assume liability for damages caused by inaccuracies in the data, and makes no warranty on the accuracy of the information contained herein. This story has not been authorized or endorsed by Kanye West.

PLB / PLB2,28,29

Kanye West puts his arm around a member of the band Justice vs. Simian as he complains about his loss onstage at the MTV Europe Music Awards.

Rapper with an Attitude

*A*nticipating yet another award, Kanye West listened for his name to be called as the winner in the Best Video category. The November 2006 MTV Europe Music Awards, held in the Danish capital of Copenhagen and hosted by Justin Timberlake, was a star-studded event. Earlier in the evening, Kanye had received the Best Hip-Hop Act award.

The announcement came at last. The award for Best Video went to Justice vs. Simian for "We Are Your Friends." An outraged Kanye bum-rushed the stage. Spouting expletives, he complained that his music video, "Touch the Sky," should have won because it "cost a million dollars, Pamela Anderson was in it. I was jumping across canyons." He added, "If I don't win, the awards show loses credibility."

Later, he told the Associated Press, "It didn't get any nominations, but it's one of the most memorable videos of the year for me." The media called Kanye a sore loser and compared his November meltdown to a similar outburst in 2004 when he complained backstage that he was robbed because he didn't win a trophy. In 2007, the rapper lashed out when he was overlooked for opening the MTV Video Music Awards. "Maybe my skin's not right," he said. When he did not win any of the three awards for which he was nominated, he stated he would not come back to MTV ever again.

Outspoken and controversial, Kanye's inflated ego gave him the confidence to defy hip-hop stereotypes—it also became a large part of his public personality. "I do music for the sake of showing off," he told *Spin*. Though his arrogance

Kanye teamed up with hip-hop violinist Miri Ben Ari to perform at the 32nd Annual American Music Awards in 2004.

alienated people, he admitted, "I worry more about not being myself."

When media worldwide criticized his behavior, Kanye paid comedian Zach Galifianakis to make a video spoof of Kanye's song "Can't Tell Me Nothing." "I think that it was a good way to present the music, especially coming off of the backlash and negative press that I was getting from what I did onstage on that European awards show," he said in *Interview*.

Not that the artist hasn't been recognized. He has received over 100 award nominations and taken home dozens of wins. Still, the rapper's overconfidence became synonymous with his name, a trait that earned kudos as often as criticism.

When he was college-aged, Kanye's production skills, his work as a rapper, vocalist, and percussion and piano musician got the attention of Columbia Studios. The record label sent a limousine to shuttle him to their office to talk about a contract.

> *Meeting with Columbia Records executive Michael Mauldin, Kanye boasted that he would be bigger than superstar Michael Jackson.*

Meeting with Columbia Records executive Michael Mauldin, Kanye boasted that he would be bigger than superstar Michael Jackson or Atlanta producer and rapper Jermaine Dupri.

The contract never materialized. Kanye may have offended Mauldin. At the time of his boasting, Kanye did not know that Mauldin was Dupri's father. The experience strengthened the rapper's determination to make it to the top in the entertainment industry.

Kanye's attitude and interest in hip-hop music showed up at a young age. At school talent shows, he said, "I would help the others because I just knew I was going to win anyway. The teachers used to say, 'This ain't meant to be the Kanye West Show.'"

In 1997, he coproduced several cuts on fellow rapper Mase's album *Harlem World*. A writer and producer, his career took off in 2000 when he produced "This Can't Be Life" for Jay-Z's *Dynasty: Roc La Familia* album, and composed three more songs for him: "Izzo H.O.V.A." (2001), " '03 Bonnie Clyde" (2002), and "Encore" (2003). In demand as a producer, he worked with Twista, Ludacris, and Alicia Keys.

In 2005, Kanye received nine Grammy nominations, eight for his first solo project, *The College Dropout*. He took home Grammy Awards for Best Rap Song, Best R&B Song, and Best Rap Album. When *The College Dropout* became a double-platinum, triple-Grammy success, many in the industry were surprised. But not Kanye.

Some called him arrogant. In the lyrics of "Last Call," Kanye responded that he used "arrogance as the steam to power my dreams." He told *Jet* magazine, "I always say you have to be a little postal to push the envelope."

Kanye's flamboyance made for good press— and lots of it. Yet his rapid rise to Grammy Award level was not without personal challenges and painful personal loss.

College Dropout

Kanye Omari West was born on June 8, 1977, in Atlanta, Georgia. In the African language of Swahili, Kanye (pronounced KON-yay) means "the only one."

His father, Ray West, earned two master's degrees and was a member of the Black Panthers, an African-American civil rights organization that was active from the mid-1960s into the 1970s. As one of the first black photojournalists for the *Atlanta Journal-Constitution*, Ray was an award-winning photographer who later became a Christian marriage counselor. Kanye's mother, Dr. Donda West, was a professor of English at Clark Atlanta University and would become Chair of the English Department at Chicago State University.

Kanye's parents separated when he was eleven months old. They divorced when he was three years old, and Kanye and his mother moved to Chicago, Illinois. Though he lived mostly with his mother, he often spent summers in Maryland with his father. "I was really raised in the church, and raised as a good Black man," he told *Ebony*. Both sides of his family were involved in activism. His father taught him to be race

It was an award-winning night in 2005 when Kanye collected trophies for Best R&B Song, Best Rap Song, and Best Rap Album at the 47th Annual Grammy Awards.

conscious. His mother taught him a wide vocabulary through word games. "I was taught to think on my own," he said in the *New York Daily News*. "That's what a lot of black kids don't get."

Kanye mixed socially conscious lyrics with commercial party beats. He told *Spin* in 2004, "I'm one of the only rappers who has both his parents and all his grandparents still alive. My father was a Black Panther. My grandparents were involved in civil-rights marches. So I have a responsibility to reflect them."

In Chicago, Kanye grew up in an upper-middle-class environment. When he was ten years old, he accompanied his mother to China, where she taught English at a university in Nanjing for a year. Kanye learned the Chinese language well enough to interpret for his mother in restaurants. "I think that got me ready to be a celeb because, at that time, a lot of Chinese had never seen a black person," he told the *Daily Telegraph*. "They would come up and stare at me, rub my skin, fishbowl me." He wrote his first raps around this time and made money by break-dancing on the streets.

A few years after returning from China, Kanye decided to design video games. "For a video game, you need a design program and characters and movement and animation and background and music," he listed. "So my mother's helping me get all these programs. And I remember the day, back in seventh grade, getting the sound program and going home and getting hooked onto it." He spent hours in his room rapping and beatmaking.

"I never had to worry about 'Where's Kanye?' " Donda said, "because he was sitting right there in front of that keyboard."

While attending Polaris High School in suburban Oak Lawn, Illinois, Kanye became friends with producer No I.D., who was working with rapper Common before he became famous. After high school, Kanye attended the American Academy of Art in Chicago on scholarship. Next, he attended Chicago State University as an English major but spent most of his time "in music class or in the lunch room talking with girls," he said. His grades were poor and he dropped out.

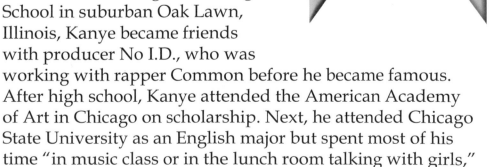

"I think that got me ready to be a celeb because, at that time, a lot of Chinese had never seen a black person."

While in school, Kanye produced songs for Chicago rappers, developing Midwest rap. He made a name for himself by producing hit singles for major hip-hop artists, including Alicia Keys, Cam'ron, Janet Jackson, Jay-Z, John Legend, Mobb Deep, Paul Wall, Scarface, Talib Kweli, and The Game. Working with Roc-A-Fella in the late 1990s, he was the go-to producer for hot tracks for the label's artists and albums.

From 2001 to 2004, he moved from hip-hop beatmaker to worldwide hitmaker. Working with the Roc-A-Fella label, he wanted to rap, not just produce. He asked the Roc-A-Fella executives to let him record his own album. They refused.

In 2002, Kanye fell asleep at the wheel of his Lexus. The accident nearly cost him his life.

"We all grew up street guys who had to do whatever we had to do to get by," Jay-Z told *Time*. "Then there's Kanye, who to my knowledge has never hustled a day in his life. I didn't see how it could work."

"I was mad because I was not being taken seriously as a rapper for a long time," Kanye said in the *Chicago Tribune*. "Whether it was because I didn't have a larger-than-life persona, or I was perceived as the guy who made beats, I was disrespected as a rapper."

In October 2002, after a late-night production session in Los Angeles, Kanye fell asleep at the wheel of his Lexus. The accident nearly cost him his life. He recalled intense pain and the sensation of his face slamming into the steering wheel,

It was a night to celebrate for Kanye and his mother, Donda West, when his sophomore project, Late Registration, *collected awards for Best Rap Performance, Best Rap Song, and Best Rap Album.*

breaking his jaw in three places. His recovery required reconstructive surgery.

"Being that I was so close to dying, I realized that nothing in life is promised except death," Kanye said in *Ebony*. "So while I'm here, I have to make the most of it."

During his rehabilitation, he used a drum machine to generate beats while he recorded mumbled vocals through his wired jaw about his experience. "Through the Wire" convinced the record label that he could rap as well as produce, and he began to record his album.

"Death is the best thing that can ever happen to a rapper," Kanye told *Time*. "Almost dying isn't bad either."

Graduation

*T*hough she had hoped her son would earn several degrees, Donda West supported Kanye's choice to pursue a career in the music industry. "It was drummed into my head that college is the ticket to a good life," Donda told the *Chicago Tribune.* "But some career goals don't require college. For Kanye to make an album called *College Dropout,* it was more about having the guts to embrace who you are, rather than following the path society has carved out for you. And that's what Kanye did."

The release date for the album was pushed back again and again. Then advance tracks of the album were leaked. Kanye outsmarted the pirates by remixing the contents and adding tracks. *The College Dropout,* finally released in February 2004, was a collection of complex songs that were a fresh deviation from the violence of most hip-hop artists. "I never killed anybody, so I don't rap about it," he said. "Every song is an inspirational song, to make you feel good."

The College Dropout was also a venue for Kanye to mouth off and get the last word. *The New York Times* reviewed that the project "taunts everyone who didn't believe in him: teachers, record executives, police officers, even his former boss at the Gap."

Certified triple platinum, *The College Dropout* defined his style, featuring wordplay and sampling. "My CD is so good," he said in the *New York Daily News*, "people will have to buy second and third copies because other people will be stealing them."

Keeping the teddy bear mascot from *The College Dropout* as his logo, by 2005, Kanye founded his own record label, G.O.O.D. (Getting Out Our Dreams). John Legend and Common were the first two artists to sign with the new label. Meanwhile, Kanye used part of his mounting wealth to finance his father's Good Water Store and Café in Lexington Park, Maryland. The *Good* in the café's name has the same meaning as Kanye's music label. The store offers water in three grades of purity, and, true to the family's activist roots, spurs awareness of global clean-water issues.

Keeping the teddy bear mascot from The College Dropout as his logo, by 2005, Kanye founded his own record label, G.O.O.D. (Getting Out Our Dreams).

Coming off the success of his first album, Kanye had to face his fear. "I'm scared of failure," he told *Entertainment Weekly*. "I was scared to work on the second album, but I have eight people in the studio while I'm working on a track and I ask them a million questions. 'What did you think of this? Do you think this is

In support of his sophomore album, Late Registration, *Kanye launched his United Kingdom tour in London in February 2006.*

it?' And I want the truth. You can't learn anything from a compliment."

West broke his production budget and spent $2 million on his second album *Late Registration*—but it sold over 860,000 copies in the first week. " 'Heard 'Em Say' is my favorite song of all time that I ever did," he said in *Entertainment Weekly*. *Spin* reviewed his triple-platinum project, calling it "as ornate and bloated as West's ego."

After a successful career in education, Donda resigned to become her son's manager. The change in career from professor to the music industry was "a huge learning curve," she said in *Jet*. Mother and son cofounded the Kanye West Foundation to help combat the severe dropout problem in high schools nationwide. As part of the foundation, Loop Dreams was designed to use students' interest in hip-hop culture to help them develop skills, express themselves creatively, and be empowered.

> **Kanye and his mother shared an undeniable bond. On his Late Registration album, Kanye sang a tribute to Donda in "Hey Mama."**

Kanye and his mother shared an undeniable bond. On his *Late Registration* album, Kanye sang a tribute to Donda in "Hey Mama." The lyrics described his mother as a single parent who worked hard to provide for him.

In 2007, Kanye released his third solo project, *Graduation*. "What I'm saying with *Graduation* is that I've graduated—nothing is holding me back anymore," he told *Interview*. "I

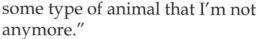

can use the Internet to directly communicate with the fans — who are the people that I need to communicate with — so no one can put up a façade around me or make me out to be some type of animal that I'm not anymore."

In May of 2007, Donda released a memoir, *Raising Kanye: Life Lessons from the Mother of a Hip-Hop Superstar*. "He told me, 'There's no real acrimony between us — there's no controversy.' He didn't think people would buy [the book]," Donda told the *Chicago Tribune*. "But I felt there are a lot of things about Kanye and me that might be beneficial to other mothers and their children."

Donda was Kanye's biggest cheerleader. "I've always worshipped the ground he walked on," she said in *Rolling Stone*. "People could say I spoiled Kanye. I don't think so. He was very much indulged." A Fulbright Scholar, Donda chaired the Kanye West Foundation and was chief executive of West Brands, the parent company of her son's businesses. She appeared at many of her son's events, including his thirtieth birthday party in New York, and his appearance on *The Oprah Winfrey Show*. On all his albums, Kanye wove in references to his mother.

Then, on November 10, 2007, at age fifty-eight, Donda suddenly died. Her death may have resulted from complications following cosmetic surgery involving a tummy tuck and breast reduction procedure.

> "I've always worshipped the ground he walked on," Donda said. "People could say I spoiled Kanye. I don't think so."

Donda West's book, Raising Kanye: Life Lessons from the Mother of a Hip-Hop Superstar, *was published in May 2007. Donda passed away six months later.*

In London at the time of his mother's death, Kanye was devastated by the news. Donda's funeral was held in Oklahoma City on November 20. During his first performance after her burial and at every date on his Glow in the Dark tour, Kanye dedicated a performance of "Hey Mama" and Journey's "Don't Stop Believing" to his mother.

Kanye's life would be forever altered without his mother. He had to carry on without his greatest fan.

Style and Controversy

Kanye's middle-class background and preppy dress made him seem out of place for the hip-hop scene dominated by gangsta personalities. "Kanye wore a pink shirt with the collar sticking up and Gucci loafers," Damon Dash, then CEO of Roc-A-Fella, told *Time*. His fashion sense set him apart from his rapper peers. Kanye was named best dressed several times, including by *Esquire* in 2005.

His production style wove pitched-up song samples with his own drums and instruments. *Late Registration* incorporated snippets of music by a wide variety of artists. He built "Diamonds from Sierra Leone" on a sample of Shirley Bassey's theme song from the James Bond film *Diamonds Are Forever*.

"I'm pretty calculating," he told *Time*. "I take stuff that I know appeals to people's bad sides and match it up with stuff that appeals to their good sides."

His 2004 single "Jesus Walks," for example, went against conventional opinion that any song about God would not get commercial radio play. Kanye stated that if the Bible were being written in the present day, he is famous and important enough to be included in it. In January 2006, he appeared on the cover of *Rolling Stone* magazine in the image of Jesus wearing a crown of thorns. He said, "I throw up historical subjects in a way that makes kids want to learn about them."

With *Graduation*, Kanye employed do-it-yourself guerrilla-style marketing. He leaked tracks online and shot his own videos. "That's the only way you can connect with people," he said in *Interview*. "If it's about being a 'street' rapper—well, the new 'street' is the Internet. So you have to embrace that culture. That's the way I got here, breaking the boundaries—and that's the way I'm going to stay here."

Kanye's history of speaking out includes criticizing President George W. Bush. On September 2, 2005, five days after Hurricane Katrina devastated New Orleans and many towns on the Gulf Coast, Kanye spoke at *A Concert for Hurricane Relief* on NBC. He deviated from the script when he said, "I hate the way they portray us in the media. You see a black family, it says, 'They're looting.' You see a white family, it says, 'They're looking for food.' It's been five days because most of the people are black. Even for me to complain about it, I would be a hypocrite because I've tried to turn away from the TV, because it's too hard to watch. I've even been shopping before even giving a donation, so I'm calling my business manager right now to see what's the biggest amount I can give." When Kanye spoke again, he said, "George Bush doesn't care about black people."

> **"If it's about being a 'street' rapper—well, the new 'street' is the Internet. So you have to embrace that culture."**

In a friendly faceoff between Kanye and 50 Cent, the two rappers topped Billboard's album charts when they released their albums on the same day, with top sales going to Kanye's Graduation.

He has also criticized blacks for being homophobic. "I actually think that standing up for gays was even more crazy than bad-mouthing the president," he told *Entertainment Weekly*.

To create a marketing opportunity, Kanye moved the release date of his third album, *Graduation*, from September 18 to September 11 to coincide with fellow rapper 50 Cent's release of his album, *Curtis*. The event was hyped as an epic battle of rap titans. 50 Cent declared that he would stop making solo albums if Kanye outsold him, but retracted the statement when *Graduation*'s first week of sales totaled 957,000 to *Curtis*'s 691,000. Kanye had definitely established himself as a rapper as well as a producer.

Giving Back

*A*s his career skyrocketed, Kanye participated in efforts encouraging young African Americans to vote. Charities to which he contributes include Food Bank for New York City, Habitat For Humanity, Kanye West Foundation, Live 8, Live Earth, MusiCares, Red Cross, and The Lunchbox Fund. His song "Jesus Walks" has become a staple at his benefit concerts.

He performed at the Live 8 concert to raise awareness about poverty and debt in the Third World. After Hurricane Katrina struck the Gulf Coast of the United States, Kanye contributed to a CD compilation benefiting victims of the massive storm.

On March 25, 2007, Kanye joined his father in Lexington Park, Maryland, for a Walk for Water rally and to promote the Good Water Store and Café. Celebrating World Water Day, the event symbolized the effort many people around the world must make to gather water daily.

Following his mother's death, Kanye scheduled a charity concert and VIP event to raise funds for the Kanye West

"Jesus Walks" is a favorite of Kanye's to perform at benefit concerts, such as Kenny Smith's Hurricane Katrina Relief NBA Charity Game on September 11, 2005, in Houston, Texas.

Foundation. Held at Chicago's House of Blues, the event included a VIP reception and silent auction of Kanye West memorabilia. He and the rest of the family also requested that donations be made in Dr. West's name to the Loop Dreams Teacher Training Institute.

Many years after Kanye's overly confident meeting with Columbia executive Michael Mauldin when the promised contract did not appear, the artist had produced songs for more than 40 artists, including Beanie Sigel, DMX, Foxy Brown, and Monica. On his resume is a 1998 project titled *Life in 1472* for an Atlanta producer and recording star named Jermaine Dupri.

Looking ahead, Kanye said, "My greatest talent, more so than being a rapper, is the ability to produce, to grab things that seem like they don't belong and put them together. I love

Kanye performs at the Brooklyn Ball at the Brooklyn Museum in April 2008. The event celebrated the opening of an exhibit by Takashi Murakami, the anime artist who created the cover for Graduation.

Held in ten cities on four continents, the Live 8 concerts were designed to pressure political leaders to commit to end poverty in Africa. Kanye performed at the Live 8 concert in Philadelphia, Pennsylvania.

building things, all the labor and refining and fine-tuning. My favorite thing in the world is postproduction."

He continued, "When I'm working, when I'm creating my gifts for the world, I want it to be good. I'm like the guy in [the movie] *The Aviator* [about legendary director, aviator, and eccentric multimillionaire Howard Hughes]. They already made a movie about my life story. At some point, I'm getting out of the rap biz. Maybe in three years, I'll be a movie producer. Maybe I'll act sometimes, in Spike Lee or Quentin Tarantino movies. But it would be a shame for me to stop making music, because I'm just so good." He summarized, "I feel like I'm too busy writing history to read it."

As music reviewer Jason Birchmeier noted, "West shattered certain stereotypes about rappers. Whether it was his appearance or his rhetoric, or even just his music, this young man became a superstar on his own terms, and his singularity no doubt is part of his appeal to a great many people, especially those who don't generally consider themselves rap listeners."

"My greatest talent, more so than being a rapper, is the ability to produce, to grab things that seem like they don't belong and put them together."

"I am the number one human being in music," Kanye said on the radio show of New York personality Wendy Williams. "That means any person living or breathing is number two. Bow in the presence of greatness, family."

1977 Kanye Omari West is born on June 8 to Donda and Ray West.

c. 1987 He goes with his mother to Nanjing while she teaches there for a year.

c. 1995 He graduates from Polaris High School in Illinois.

c. 1996 He begins producing for Chicago rappers. After attending the American Academy of Art and Chicago State University, he drops out of college.

1997 Kanye coproduces several songs on Mase's album *Harlem World*.

2000 He produces "This Can't Be Life" for Jay-Z's album *Dynasty: Roc La Familia*, released in October.

2001 Kanye's career takes off when his sound is featured on Jay-Z's album *The Blueprint*.

2002 He is signed by Roc-A-Fella Records. On October 23, he suffers a near fatal car crash. He records "Through the Wire."

2004 His first solo album, *The College Dropout*, is released in February. He receives nine Grammy nominations.

2005 Kanye founds his own record label, G.O.O.D. (Getting Out Our Dreams). He headlines the second day of the Lollapalooza music festival in his hometown of Chicago on August 5. His second album, *Late Registration*, is released on August 30. On September 2, he is the featured speaker at a benefit concert on NBC, *Concert for Hurricane Relief*.

2006 On November 2, "Touch the Sky" fails to win Best Video at the MTV Europe Music Awards. He goes onstage, arguing that his video should have won. On November 7, he publicly apologizes for the outburst. In December, Robert "Evel" Knievel sues Kanye for trademark infringement in his video for "Touch the Sky."

2007 It is announced that Kanye will star in a television series directed by Larry Charles. Kanye and his father support World Water Day with a Walk for Water rally. In July, Kanye changes the release date of *Graduation* from September 18 to September 11, the same release date as 50 Cent's album *Curtis*. Kanye is nominated for eight Grammy Awards. On November 10, Donda West dies.

2008 Kanye takes home four Grammy Awards: Best Rap Album for *Graduation*, Best Rap Song for "Good Life," Best Rap Solo Performance for "Stronger," and Best Rap Performance by a Duo or Group for "Southside." In April, Kanye breaks up with Alexis Phifer, who has been his girlfriend since 2002. Fans flock to his United States spring tour. He is featured on Estelle's single "American Boy." "Love Lockdown" from his November release *808s & Heartbreak* is an instant hit.

DISCOGRAPHY

Albums

2008 *808s & Heartbreak*

2007 *Graduation*

2005 *Late Registration*

2004 *The College Dropout*

Singles

2008 "Love Lockdown"
"Heartless"

2007 "Classic"
"Can't Tell Me Nothing"
"Stronger"
"Good Life"
"Flashing Lights"

2005 "Diamonds from Sierra Leone"
"Gold Digger"
"Heard 'Em Say"
"Touch the Sky"
"Drive Slow"

2004 "Slow Jamz"
"Through the Wire"
"All Falls Down"
"Jesus Walks"
"The New Workout Plan"
"Talk About Our Love"

PHOTO CREDITS: Cover—Eric Ryan/Getty Images; p. 4—Dave Hogan/Getty Images for MTV; p. 6—Frank Micelotta/Getty Images; p. 10—Carlo Allegri/Getty Images; p. 13—Steve Granitz Archive I/WireImage for The Recording Academy/Getty Images; p. 16—Jo Hale/Getty Images; p. 19—Vince Bucci/Getty Images; p. 22—Brad Barket/Getty Images; p. 24—Joe Murphy/NBAE via Getty Images; p. 25—Theo Wargo/WireImage/Getty Images; p. 26—William Thomas Cain/Getty Images

Books

Bankston, John. *Jay-Z*. Hockessin, Delaware: Mitchell Lane Publishers, 2005

Boone, Mary. *50-Cent*. Hockessin, Delaware: Mitchell Lane Publishers, 2007.

Simons, Rae. *Kanye West*. Broomall, Pennsylvania: Mason Crest, 2007.

Tracy, Kathleen. *Justin Timberlake*. Hockessin, Delaware: Mitchell Lane Publishers, 2008.

Works Consulted

Associated Press. "Kanye West Says Best Video Didn't Get VMA Nod; He Calls His 'Touch the Sky' Video 'One of the Most Memorable' of the Year." August 30, 2006. http://www.msnbc.msn.com/id/14591428

Birchmeier, Jason. "Kanye West Biography." *Allmusic*. 2008. http://wc01.allmusic.com/cg/ amg.dll?p=amg&searchlink=KANYE

Carmanica, Jon. "Kanye West, 'Late Registration' (Roc-A-Fella/Def Jam) Hip-hop's Golden Boy Tries to Hang On to His Ego." *Spin*. September 2005.

Carter, Kelley L. "Kanye West's Mom Dies: Former Chicago State Professor, Department Head Was Inspiration, Son's Biggest Fan." *Chicago Tribune*. November 12, 2007.

Christian, Margena A. "Why Everybody Is Talking About Producer-turned-rapper Kanye West." *Jet*, January 31, 2005. http://findarticles.com/p/articles/mi_m1355/is_5_107/ai_n10300882

Ehrlich, Dimitri. "Kanye West: First Came the Acclaim, and Then the Inevitable Backlash. Now Kanye West is Out to Reinvent Himself as a Man of the World. But Is the World Ready for What He's Got in Store?" *Interview*, October 2007.

Jones, Steve. "Kanye Outduels 50 Cent." *USA Today*, September 20, 2007.

Mistri, Rishad. "Kanye West. Kanye West Has Success Written All Over Him." *Spin*, February 9, 2004. http://spinmagazine.com/articles/kanye-west

MTV News Staff. "Kanye Celebrates His 30th With Jay-Z, Fall Out Boy; Plus Andre 3000, Harry Potter, Shrek, U2 & More In For The Record." *MTV News*, June 8, 2007. http://www.mtv.com/news/articles/1562034/20070608/west_kanye.jhtml

Ogunnaike, Lola. "Kanye West World. A Nerdy Midwestern Kid Braces to Become America's Most Provocative Pop Star." *Rolling Stone*, January 25, 2006. http://www.rollingstone.com/news/coverstory/kanye_west_world

Sanneh, Kelefa. "Critic's Choice/New CD's; No Reading and Writing, But Rapping Instead." *New York Times*, February 9, 2004. http://query.nytimes.com/gst/fullpage.html?res=9B05E6DF173AF93AA35751C0A9629C8B63

Toure. "Head of the Class. Kanye West Is the Hottest Rapper Around." *Rolling Stone*, April 7, 2004. http://www.rollingstone.com/artists/kanyewest/articles/story/5940044/head_of_the_class

Tunison, Michael. "How'd You Like Your Water? At St. Mary's Cafe, to Splurge Is to Sip 99.9% Pure." *Washington Post*, December 7, 2006, page B01. http://www.washingtonpost.com/wp-dyn/content/article/2006/12/06/AR2006120602139.html

Tyrangiel, Josh. "Why You Can't Ignore Kanye." *Time*, August 21, 2005. http://www.time.com/time/magazine/article/0,9171,1096499,00.html

Valby, Karen. "The Ego Has Landed: With Eight Grammy Nominations and a Beloved Second Album, Kanye West Is on Fire. So Why Does the World's Cockiest Rapper Sound So Nervous?" *Entertainment Weekly*, February 3, 2006.

Vibe. "Living the Good Life," January 2008. page 67.

On the Internet

Kanye West Official Site
www.kanyewest.com

Roc-A-Fella Records
www.rocafella.com